SO FUNNY YOU'LL PUKE

Why do blondes take the pill?
  So they can remember what day it is.

What do Vietnamese consider a seven-course meal?
  Six puppies and a pound of rice.

How many perverts does it take to screw in a lightbulb?
  Just one—but it takes the entire emergency room to get it out.

What do you call a woman with no arms or legs holding a coat?
  Peg.

How do you get rid of unwanted pubic hair?
  Spit.

BOOK YOUR PLACE ON OUR WEBSITE AND MAKE THE READING CONNECTION!

We've created a customized website just for our very special readers, where you can get the inside scoop on everything that's going on with Zebra, Pinnacle and Kensington books.

When you come online, you'll have the exciting opportunity to:

- View covers of upcoming books

- Read sample chapters

- Learn about our future publishing schedule (listed by publication month *and author*)

- Find out when your favorite authors will be visiting a city near you

- Search for and order backlist books from our online catalog

- Check out author bios and background information

- Send e-mail to your favorite authors

- Meet the Kensington staff online

- Join us in weekly chats with authors, readers and other guests

- Get writing guidelines

- AND MUCH MORE!

**Visit our website at
http://www.kensingtonbooks.com**

TWISTEDLY GROSS JOKES

VOLUME XXXIV

Julius Alvin

PINNACLE BOOKS
Kensington Publishing Corp.
http://www.kensingtonbooks.com

PINNACLE BOOKS are published by

Kensington Publishing Corp.
850 Third Avenue
New York, NY 10022

All Kensington Titles, Imprints, and Distributed Lines are available at special quantity discounts for bulk purchases for sales promotions, premiums, fund-raising, and educational or institutional use. Special book excerpts or customized printings can also be created to fit specific needs. For details, write or phone the office of the Kensington special sales manager: Kensington Publishing Corp., 850 Third Avenue, New York, NY 10022, attn: Special Sales Department, Phone: 1-800-221-2647.

Pinnacle and the P logo Reg. U.S. Pat. & TM Off.

First Printing: December 2001
10 9 8 7 6 5 4 3 2 1

Printed in the United States of America

CONTENTS

Now That's Gross

A young guy is speeding across a bridge in his fancy sports car. Sure enough, a cop with a radar gun is sitting on the other side of the bridge. The cop pulls him over, then walks up to the guy's car and asks, "What's the hurry?"

The guy replies, "I'm late for work, Officer."

"What do you do?"

"Well, I'm a rectum stretcher."

"What? A rectum stretcher?"

The guy explains, "Yeah. I start with a finger, then work my way up to two fingers. Eventually I get a hand in, then both hands, and I slowly stretch it until it's about six feet wide."

The curious cop asks, "What do you do with a six-foot asshole?"

The guy answers, "Well, you give him a radar gun and park him at the end of a bridge."

Two guys immigrated to America. On their first day off the boat, they were wandering around New York City, seeing the sights. As lunchtime approached, they decided they were hungry. They came up to a street vendor selling hot dogs.

One said to the other, in a shocked tone, "My God. Do they eat dogs in America?"

"I don't know!" said the other, equally appalled.

"Well," said the first, "we're going to be Americans, so we must do as they do."

They approached the vendor bravely, and said, "Two hot dogs, please."

The vendor handed them their food in a pair of paper sacks, and the two immigrants sat on a park bench to eat their lunch. One looked inside his sack, hesitated, and turned to his partner and said, "Uhh, which part of the dog did you get?"

––––––––––––––

Two girls, a blonde and a brunette, are walking down the street and pass a flower shop, where the brunette happens to see her boyfriend buying flowers. She sighs and says, "Oh, crap, my boyfriend is buying me flowers again. For no reason."

The blonde looks quizzically at her and says, "What's the big deal? Don't you like getting flowers?"

The brunette says, "Oh, sure . . . but he always has expectations after getting me flowers, and I just don't feel like spending the next three days on my back with my legs in the air."

The blonde says, "Don't you have a vase?"

––––––––––––––

A man walked into a bar and ordered a beer. He drank half and then poured the rest on his hand.

A few minutes later, the man ordered another beer and the bartender became suspicious.

Again, the man drank half and then poured the rest on his hand.

A short while later, the man ordered yet another beer.

The bartender finally asked, "Excuse me, sir, but what the heck are you doing?"

The irritated guy replied, "Can't you see that my date and I are trying to have a drink?"

———————————————

John was in a bar looking very dejected. His friend, Steve, walked over and asked, "What's wrong?"

"It's my mother-in-law," John replied, shaking his head sadly. "I have a real problem with her."

"Cheer up," Steve said. "Everyone has problems with their mother-in-law."

"Yeah," John answered. "But not everybody gets theirs pregnant."

———————————

Why did Japan send us 50 million cases of Viagra?

They heard that our entire country can't get an election.

———————————

A boy said to his father one day, "Dad, when I grow up I want to be a musician."

His father responded, "I'm sorry, son, you can't have it both ways."

_____

Why is a government worker like a shotgun with a broken firing pin?

It won't work and you can't fire it.

_____

Al Gore and George W. Bush found themselves in the same barbershop at the same time, seated side by side, getting the works.

Their barbers finished shaving the two presidential candidates at about the same time, and each barber reached for some aftershave to slap on his customer's face.

Gore shouted, "Hey, don't put that stuff on me! My wife will think I've been in a whorehouse!"

Bush said calmly to his barber, "Go ahead and put it on. My wife doesn't know what the inside of a whorehouse smells like."

Husband: Shall we try a different position tonight?

Wife: That's a good idea. Why don't you stand at the sink and do dishes and I'll sit on the sofa and fart.

———————————

A pretty blond woman is driving down a country road in Arkansas in her new sports car, when something goes wrong with the car and it breaks down.

Luckily, she happens to be near a house. She goes up to it and knocks. When a lady answers the door, she says to her, "Oh, it's Sunday night and my car broke down! I don't know what to do! Can I stay here for the night until tomorrow when I can get some help?"

"Well," drawls the lady, "you can stay here,

but I don't want you messin' with my sons Bill and Roger."

She looks through the screen door and sees two very young men standing behind the lady. She judges them to be in their late teens. "Okay," she says.

After everyone has gone to bed for the night, the woman begins to think about the two boys in the room next to hers. So she quietly goes into their room and says, "Boys, how would you like for me to teach you the ways of the world?"

They say, "Sure."

She says, "The only thing is, I don't want to get pregnant, so you have to wear these condoms."

She puts them on the boys, and the three of them go at it all night long.

Five years later, Bill and Roger are sitting on the front porch, rocking back and forth. Bill says, "Roger?"

Roger says, "Yeah, Bill?"

Bill says, "You remember that blond woman that came by here about five years ago and showed us the ways of the world?"

"Yeah," says Roger, "I remember."

"Well, do you care if she gets pregnant?" asks Bill.

"Nope," says Roger, "I reckon not."

"Me neither," says Bill. "Let's take these things off."

A guy is walking down a street in Vegas, and he's really horny. So he goes to the first whorehouse he sees. He only has five dollars, so they kick him out.

The guy goes to the next one, but since he only has five dollars, he gets kicked out again.

So by this time, he's super horny, so he goes to the next one and says, "Look, I only have five dollars. I'm really horny, and I need a blow job for five dollars!"

The guy there says, "Okay. For five dollars, we can give you a penguin."

"What's a penguin?"

"You'll see."

So, the guy takes the five dollars and leads the horny man to a bedroom. The horny man unzips his pants and waits for his "penguin." Soon a whore comes in and starts giving the guy a blow job. Just as he's about to let loose, she stops and walks away.

Now the horny guy, with his pants at his ankles, waddles after her, shouting, "Hey! What's a penguin?"

———————————

Why do blondes take the pill?
    Just so they know what day of the week it is.

———————————

What is the best way to stop an Iraqi tank attack?
    Shoot the soldiers that are pushing them.

———————————

How can you tell there has been a blonde in your refigerator?
    There is lipstick on your cucumbers.

———————————

What is the Jewish concept of perfect sex?
   Simultaneous headaches.

_____

What is the object of a Jewish football game?
   To get the quarter back.

_____

Why do Jewish American Princesses close their eyes while having sex?
   So they can fantasize that they're shopping.

_____

Did you hear about the paternity suit against Michael Jackson?

He denies that he's the father, but still wants visitation rights.

———————————

How do you get a female Arkansan into an elevator?

First grease up the doorway, then throw in a Twinkie.

———————————

What do Vietnamese consider a seven-course meal?
   Six puppies and a pound of rice.

_____

What does a black kid get for his fourth birthday present?
   A switchblade.

_____

What does a black kid get for his eighth birthday present?
   Laid.

_____

What does a black kid get for his tenth birthday present?
   Fatherhood.

_____

What does a black kid get for his eighteenth birthday present?
   Bailed out.

_____

What do you get when you cross a Caucasian man and a Thai woman?
   Syphilis.

_____

What is the quickest way to make a Mexican forget his English?
Offer him a job.

———————————

Have you seen the new Asian bumper sticker?
It says *I'd rather be driving*.

———————————

A woman woke up and told her husband about a dream she'd just had. "I was at an auction for penises. The big ones sold for a thousand dollars and the tiny ones for ten."
The husband asked, "What about one my size?"
The wife replied, "Didn't even get a bid!"
Pissed off and wanting revenge, he told his

wife the next morning that he'd had a dream too. "I was at an auction for vaginas. The really tight ones sold for a thousand dollars and the loose ones for ten."

So the wife asked, "What about ones like mine?"

The husband replied, "That's where they held the auction."

———————

How can you tell if the house you're at belongs to a faggot?

The welcome mat reads *Wipe your knees.*

———————

So Gross Even
We're Offended

Why did the fag go to the costume party covered in whipped cream?

He told everyone he was supposed to be a wet dream.

A small company was on the edge of bankruptcy. The owner summoned his two-man sales force into his office. "Things aren't going too well, guys," he announced grimly. "So to perk up sales I'm announcing a contest. The guy with the most sales gets a blow job."

"What does the loser get?" asked one of the salesmen.

The owner looked at both men and said, "The loser gets to give it."

Why do women have orgasms?

It gives them one extra reason to moan.

A lawyer went on vacation to a western dude ranch. Awed by the scenery, he took a twilight stroll among the cattle. Suddenly, he stepped in a huge pile of horseshit.

"Oh, no!" he shouted. "I'm melting!"

over at Gary and, shaking her head, whispers, "What a hypocrite you are. You spent most of last night with your face full of hair."

Gary says, "Yeah? Well, how long do you think I'd have stayed if I found a piece of spaghetti in there?"

————————————

Boy That's Gross

Why do men pay more than women for car insurance?

Because women don't get blow jobs while they're driving.

Things Guys Shouldn't Say
After Having Sex

I was kidding about being sterile, you know.

Do you always fart like that when someone shoves it in?

How come it's so *big* in there?

You've done this with a lotta guys before—right?

Next time I come over, don't bother with the underwear, okay?

(Sniff, sniff.) Is that *cat* food?

Okay, guys, it's a wrap, cut and print it!

You are great in bed, but your sister gives better head!

My first wife was prettier, but you can screw a lot better.

Do you know what a "douche" is?

Maybe if you did some pushups, your boobs would grow.

I want you to try some of *my* deodorant.

I'm not into relationships. Can't we just screw, like every Tuesday night or something?

Maybe if you lost some weight, I could get it all the way in!

I never saw a girl with hairy tits before!

I've been getting these little blisters lately . . .

You wanna do those dishes before you leave?

You should go wash that; the cabbie will think something *died* in there!

———————

The female office worker was thrilled to get her good-looking male coworker to agree to go home with her at the end of the day. After a bout of heavy kissing and petting she took him by the hand and led him toward the bedroom but warned him, "We have to hurry, though. My husband will be getting home from work soon."

"Oh, yeah? Getting home soon? Just how soon?"

"Oh, shit," she groaned, "not another faggot."

———————

How many perverts does it take to put in a lightbulb?

Just one, but it takes the entire emergency room to get it out.

———————————

Why did the blonde suddenly become enraged after five years of faithful service in the whorehouse?

Because she found out that the other girls were getting paid.

———————————

Twelve Reasons a Handgun is Better Than a Woman

1. You can buy a silencer for a handgun.
2. You can trade your .44 in for two .22s.
3. You can have a handgun at home and another for the road.
4. If you admire a friend's handgun and tell him so, he will be impressed and let you try it out.
5. Your primary handgun doesn't mind if you have a backup.
6. Your handgun will stay with you even if you are out of ammo.
7. A handgun doesn't take up a lot of your closet space.
8. Handguns function normally every day of the month.
9. A handgun won't ask, "Do these grips make me look fat?"
10. A handgun doesn't mind if you go to sleep right after you're done using it.

11. A handgun doesn't care how big your trigger finger is.
12. A handgun won't complain if you are a "little fast on the trigger."

————————————

What do a bowling ball and a blonde have in common?

You can pick them up, stick your fingers in them, and throw them in the gutter, and they'll always come back.

————————————

You Might Be from Alabama If . . .

1. The halloween pumpkin on your front porch has more teeth than your spouse.
2. You let your twelve-year-old daughter smoke at the table in front of her kids.
3. You have been married three times and still have the same in-laws.
4. Anyone in your family has ever died after saying, "Hey, watch this."
5. Your Junior/Senior prom had a day-care center.

———————————

Just after delivering the blonde's new baby, the doctor solemnly said to her, "I am sorry, madam, to have to inform you that your baby is not normal. It is a hermaphrodite."

The blonde replied, "I am sorry, but I don't know what a 'hermaphrodite' is."

"It means your baby has the physical characteristics of both sexes," he told her.

"Wow," she says. "You mean both a vagina and a brain?"

The young blonde approached her mother and asked, "Is it true that babies come out of the same place where boys put their thingies?"

"Yes, dear, it is," said her mother, glad that her daughter was finally communicating about sex.

"Well," the blonde replied, "then won't I risk getting all of my teeth knocked out?"

———————————

Have you heard about the new supersensitive condoms?

After the man leaves, they hang around and talk to the woman.

———————————

How do you know a blonde likes you?

She has sex with you two nights in a row.

———————————

Little Max has just been toilet trained and decides to use the big toilet like his daddy. He pushes up the seat and balances his little penis on the rim. Just then the toilet seat slams down, and Max lets out a scream.

His mother comes running to find Max hopping round the room clutching his genitals and howling. He looks up at her with his little tear-stained face and sniffles, "K—k—kiss it and make it it better."

Little Max's mother shouts, "Don't start your father's shit with me!"

———————————

What happened to the leper who visited Harlem?

Someone stole his kneecaps.

The blonde rushing through the grocery store headed for the express line. She noticed that the male checker had his back to her, so she said, "Excuse me, could you please check me out?"

He turned around, gazed at her from head to toe, and said, "Nice tits."

How does a blonde prepare for safe sex?
  She puts on rubber-based lipstick.

———————————

What did the blonde's mom say to her before
the blonde's date?
  "If you're not in bed by twelve, come
home."

———————————

What's more fun than swinging dead babies
around on a clothesline?
  Stopping them with a shovel.

———————————

What has 180 legs and no pubic hair?
   The entire front row of an 'N Sync concert.

———————————

What's blue and flies around the room at high speeds?
   A dead baby with a punctured lung.

———————————

Why do dogs always stick their noses in women's cunts?
   Because they can do it and get away with it.

———————————

Why are dogs better than kids?
    Because when you get tired of your dog, you can put him to sleep.

––––––––––––––––––––

If a black guy and a Mexican get into a fight, who wins?
    We all do.

––––––––––––––––––––

How does a Polish guy do crack?
    He swipes his finger across his asshole and sniffs.

––––––––––––––––––––

Why do female Jehovah's Witnesses have inverted nipples?

From people poking them in the tits, saying, "Get the fuck outta my house."

———————————

What do women and shrimp have in common?

The pink part is great, and they're better with their heads cut off.

———————————

How do you get rid of unwanted pubic hair?

Spit.

———————————

Just Plain Gross

What did the Ethiopian say when the skeleton fell on him?

"Get off me, you fat bastard!"

A guy goes to see his eye doctor, who tells him, "You've got to stop masturbating."

"Why? Am I going blind?" the guy asks.

"No," says the eye doctor, "but you're upsetting the other patients in the waiting room."

How can you tell when a girl is really horny?
   She sits on your open hand and it feels like
a horse eating out of your palm.

_____

Did you hear about the fag who had plastic
surgery to have his love handles removed?
   Now he has no ears.

_____

What does an 800-pound gerbil do for fun?
   He sticks homos up his ass.

_____

Where do people with one leg go for breakfast?

IHOP.

_____

Did you hear about the new Polish abortion clinic?

There's a two-year wait.

_____

A guy calls the doctor in the middle of the night and cries, "Doc, you gotta help us—our baby boy just swallowed a rubber."

The doctor leaps out of bed and gets dressed as quickly as he can. Just as he's about to leave, the phone rings again.

It's the same guy who says, "Forget it, Doc, it's okay. We found another one."

———————————

Did you hear about the Mexican college student?

Neither did I.

———————————

Why did God create women?

To carry the semen from the bedroom to the toilet.

————————————

A guy walks into a pet store and says to the clerk, "My dog just died, and I want to get another one."

The clerk says, "You don't want a dog. I have the perfect pet for you—a toothless hamster."

"What would I want with a toothless hamster?" the guy asks.

The clerk says to the guy, "I'll show you. Take out your pecker."

The guy does. The clerk opens a cage, and a hamster jumps out, attaches himself to the guys cock, and gives him the best blow job he's ever had.

"I'll take him!" the guy says, and pays for the

toothless hamster. He comes home, and when his wife sees the new pet, she shrieks, "What the hell is that?"

"Never mind what it is," the guy replies. "Just teach it how to cook and get the hell out."

A lovely young girl was employed by a clothing firm in New York. She and her widowed mother shared the same ambition: marriage to a wealthy man.

One day the girl came home from work, eyes red from crying. As soon as she entered the apartment she called, "Mom, I'm pregnant, and my boss is the father."

She began to sob uncontrollably while her mother tried to console her.

The next morning, the mother charged into the office of the boss. "You," she shouted.

"What do you plan to do about getting my daughter pregnant?"

The elegantly attired man, handsome, unmarried, and in his mid-thirties, held up his hand. "Please take a seat, Mrs. Schwartz. I'm making all the arrangements. Your daughter will have the best doctor money can buy before the baby is born. She'll be in the best hospital. Afterward, I am arranging for a trust fund for her from which she will receive a check for twenty-five hundred dollars a week."

The mother was taken aback and thought for a moment. "Tell me," she said. "God forbid, should she have a miscarriage, will you give her another chance?"

Bob works hard at the plant and spends most evenings bowling or playing basketball at the gym. His wife thinks he is pushing himself too hard, so for his birthday she takes him to a local strip club.

The doorman at the club greets them and says, "Hey, Bob! How ya doin'?"

His wife is puzzled and asks if he's been to this club before. "Oh, no," says Bob. "He's on my bowling team."

When they are seated, a waitress asks Bob if he'd like his usual Budweiser. His wife is becoming uncomfortable and says, "You must come here a lot for that woman to know you drink Budweiser."

"No, honey, she's in the ladies bowling league. We share lanes with them."

A stripper comes over to their table and throws her arms around Bob. "Hi, Bobby," she says, "want your usual table dance?"

Bob's wife, now furious, grabs her purse and storms out of the club. Bob follows and spots her getting into a cab. Before she can slam the door, he jumps in beside her and she starts screaming at him.

The cabby turns his head and says, "Looks like you picked up a real bitch tonight, Bob!"

———————————

The salesgirl at the Pink Pussycat boutique didn't bat an eye when the customer purchased an artificial vagina.

"What are you going to use it for?" she asked.

"None of your business," answered the customer, beet red and thoroughly offended.

"Relax, mister," the salesgirl said. "The only reason I'm asking is, if it's food, we don't have to charge you sales tax."

———————————

A young couple were on their way to Vegas to get married. Before getting there, the girl said to the guy that she had a confession to make—the reason that they had not been too intimate was that she was very flat-chested. If the guy wished to cancel the wedding, it would be okay with her.

The guy thought about it for a while, and said he didn't mind she was flat, and sex was not the most important thing in a marriage.

Several miles down the road, the guy turned to the girl and said that he also wanted to make a confession—he said that below his waist, "It's just like a baby." If the girl wanted to cancel the marriage, it would be okay with him.

The girl thought about it for a while and said that she didn't mind, and she also believed there were other things far more important than sex in a marriage.

Happy that they were honest with each other, they went on to Vegas and got married.

On their wedding night, the girl took off her clothes; she was as flat as a washboard. Finally, the guy took off his clothes. After one glance at the guy's naked body, the girl fainted and fell to the floor.

When she became conscious, the guy said, "I told you before we got married. Why did you still faint?"

The girl said, "You told me it was just like a baby."

The guy replied, "It is! Eight pounds and twenty one inches long!"

Adolf Hitler was conducting a general staff meeting, when somebody sneezed.

"Who vas zat?" shouted Hitler, whirling around from a wall map of Europe.

Nobody said anything.

"I see," he said. "I vill haff ten of you shot. Und maybe zen you vill tell me who schneezed, ja?"

A Gestapo agent took ten people out of the room. Shots were heard, then silence.

"I vill ask again," yelled Hitler, "who schneezed?"

Again, nobody said anything.

"Very vell," he said, "I vill haff anosser ten of you shot!"

The Gestapo agent escorted ten more people out of the room and executed them. "For ze very last time," screamed Hitler, "who schneezed?"

Finally, the guilty officer could stand no more. He stood up and said, "It vas me, mine herr. I am ze vun who schneezed."

Hitler turned to the shaking officer and said, "*Gesundheit.*"

———————————

What do you call an invisible nigger?
    A fart.

———————————

What's warm and soft when you go to bed, but hard and stiff when you wake up?
    Vomit.

———————————

A Gross Variety

What's the difference between toilet paper and toast?
    Toast is brown on both sides.

_____

How does a redneck tell the difference between a cow and a bull in the dark?
    He sticks his nose in the animal's ass. If there's a place for his tongue, it's a cow.

_____

What's the difference between a pizza and a black man?

A pizza can feed a family of four.

What's the difference between a friend and a *real* friend?

A friend will help you move. A *real* friend will help you move the bodies.

Top Five Names For Masturbating

1. Getting some air nookie
2. Shaking your fist at your ex-girlfriend
3. Releasing the hostages
4. Tickling your Elmo
5. Downloading from your own Web site

———————————

Confucius say: Man who gets kicked in testicles, left holding the bag.

———————————

Confucius say: Woman who goes to man's apartment for snack, gets titbit.

———————————

A guy sits down in a restaurant and asks for the hot chili. The waitress says, "The guy next to you got the last bowl."

He looks over and sees that the guy's finished his meal, but the chili bowl is still full. He asks, "Are you going to eat that?"

The other guy says, "No. Help yourself."

The first guy takes it and starts to eat it. When he gets about halfway down, his fork hits something. He looks down and sees a dead mouse in it, and he pukes the chili back into the bowl.

The other guy says, "That's about as far as I got too."

———————————

Charlie, an embalmer, says to his boss one day, "There's a problem with Mrs. Whittaker."

The boss says, "What's that?"

Charlie says, "I was getting her cleaned up when I noticed a jumbo shrimp sticking out of her pussy."

The boss says, "That's impossible. Show me."

They go to the table where she's lying. Charlie flips back the sheet, points, and says, "See? There's a jumbo shrimp sticking out of her pussy."

The boss takes a closer look and says, "You jerk, that's not a piece of shrimp. That's her clit."

Charlie says, "Her clit? Well, it sure tasted like shrimp."

———————————————

A guy says to his wife, "I'm in the mood for some sixty-nine."

She says, "It's that time of the month, but if you don't care, I don't care."

They go into the bedroom, and are 69'ing like mad dogs when the doorbell rings.

She says, "Answer the door."

He says, "But my face is a mess."

She says, "It's just the postman. Answer the door, and if he says anything, just tell him you were eating a jam sandwich."

He opens the door and says, "I'm sorry about my mouth, I was eating a jam sandwich."

The mailman says, "I wasn't looking at the jam on your mouth . . . I was looking at the peanut butter on your forehead."

———————————

How can you tell if your husband's dead?
    The sex is the same, but you get the remote.

———————————

How many men does it take to change a light-bulb?
    None, they just sit there in the dark and complain.

———————————

A brunette, a blonde, and a redhead are all in third grade. Who has the biggest breasts?
    The blonde, because she's eighteen.

———————————

What do a thousand battered women have in common?
    They never shut the fuck up.

_____

How many chauvinists does it take to open a beer can?
    None, because the bitch better have it open when she hands it to you.

_____

What's the definition of a woman?
    Life support for a cunt.

_____

What do you tell a woman with two black eyes?
  Nothing, you've already told her twice.

———————————

What does a woman do after she gets out of the battered women's shelter?
  The dishes, if she knows what's good for her.

———————————

Did you hear they came out with Viagra Light?
  You don't get hard enough to fuck, but you look good in a bathing suit.

———————————

Ten Reasons Why It Sucks To Be a Guy

1. If you put a woman on a pedestal and try to protect her from the rat race, you're a male chauvinist.
2. If you work too hard, there's never enough time for her. If you don't work hard enough, you're a good-for-nothing bum.
3. If she has a boring, repetitive job with low pay, it's exploitation. If you have a boring, repetitive job with low pay, you should get off your ass and get something better.
4. If you get a promotion ahead of her, it's favoritism. If she gets a promotion ahead of you, it's equal opportunity.
5. If you mention how nice she looks, it's sexual harassment. If you keep quiet, it's male indifference.
6. If you cry, you're a wimp. If you don't, you're an insensitive bastard.

7. If you thump her, it's wife-beating. If she thumps you, it's self-defense.
8. If you make a decision without consulting her, you're a chauvinist. If she makes a decision without consulting you, she's a liberated woman.
9. If you ask her to do something she doesn't enjoy, it's domination. If she asks you, it's a favor.
10. If you appreciate the female form and frilly underwear, you're a pervert. If you don't, you're gay.

———————————

Why are women like rocks?
  You skip the flat ones.

———————————

Why do women have arms?
    Do you have any idea how long it would take to lick the toilet clean?

———————————

Did you hear they've improved Viagra?
    It's so strong now that you can get a hard-on with your wife.

———————————

What does every feminist in the world need?
    A good man to smack some sense into her.

———————————

What's the best part about getting a hand job from a woman dwarf?

Your cock looks huge in her hand.

A priest gets a flat tire fixed. As the car's coming down off the lift, the priest asks the mechanic, "Are the lug nuts tight?"

The mechanic says, "Tighter than a nun's pussy."

The priest frowns and says, "You'd better give them another turn then."

What's the difference between a lawyer and an onion?
　　You cry when you cut up an onion.

——————————————

What's the difference between a lawyer and a vulture?
　　The lawyer gets frequent flyer miles.

——————————————

What's the hardest part of eating a vegetable?
　　Manipulating the wheelchair.

——————————————

Why did God put long legs on women?
    To keep their feet from smelling like fish.

_____

What is a woman doing while looking at a blank sheet of paper?
    Reading her rights.

_____

How do you know when you are getting old?
    When you start having dry dreams and wet farts.

_____

Why do black people like finger bowls in restaurants?

So they can wash the silverware before they steal it.

_____

What's small, red, and spins round at 2,000 rpm?

A baby picking its nose with a power drill.

_____

A black guy walks up to a Southerner who's playing with his pet raccoon.

Never having seen such an animal before, the black guy asks the redneck, "Hey, what kind of critter be dat?"

"It's the same as what y'all been called all your life," the redneck replies.

"No shit?" the black guy asks. "It's called a motherfucker?"

———————————

What is the difference between a Polish woman and a Bigfoot?

One is six feet tall, dirty, hairy, and smelly, and the other has really big feet.

———————————

How did the Polish woman keep her son from biting his nails?

She made him wear shoes.

———————————

Why do women have babies?
   Because it hurts and they deserve it.

A blonde goes to see her doctor because of serious abrasions on her knees.
   "Do you know what caused these injuries?" the doctor asks.
   "Well," she replies, "I've been having sex doggie style."
   "Oh, that's no problem," the doctor says. "Just roll over and do it missionary style for a while."
   "Oh, but that is a problem," the blonde says. "Every time I try it that way, my dog's breath makes me puke!"

Why do women have foreheads?
   So you have somewhere else to kiss them after you come in their mouths.

————————————

What do you call balls on a faggot?
   Mud flaps.

————————————

What is black and has twelve green tits?
   The garbage bag at a breast cancer clinic.

————————————

What is a Mexican's idea of safe sex?
   Locking the car door.

_____

What's the difference between Princess Di and Jon Benet?
   One was killed by paparazzi and the other was killed by Papa Ramsey.

_____

Did you hear about Woody Allen's latest movie?
   It's called *Honey, I Married the Kids*.

_____

What's the definition of disgusting?

Stuffing a dozen oysters into your grand-mother's cunt and sucking out thirteen.

———————————

What should you do if you see your wife stag-gering across the backyard?

Reload.

———————————

Why do Italians wear gold chains?

To remind them where to stop shaving.

———————————

What's the difference between driving and getting a blow job?
    You can only hold one beer while you're driving.

———————————

What's blue and purple and bigger than a cocktail weenie?
    Rosie O'Donnell's clit after she walks up a flight of stairs.

———————————

What tastes good on pie but not on pussy?
    Crust.

———————————

How can you tell if someone is half Catholic and half Jewish?

When he goes to confession, he takes a lawyer with him.

———————

What do you get when you cross Rogaine and Viagra?

Don King.

———————

How do you know that you've had a good blow job?

When you have to burp her to get your balls back.

———————

What's the difference between a female lawyer and a pit bull?
  Lipstick.

How do you get a bunch of Mexicans out of your house?
  Tell them a Taco Bell truck is overturned on the freeway.

How does a romance novel set in Harlem end?
  The hero gets the heroin.

How can you tell if a Polack has been drinking from the toilet?

His breath smells better.

Morris, a ninety-year-old man, lived in a retirement home. He wanted to get away from the home for a while, so he got himself a weekend pass.

He stopped in his favorite bar and sat at the end and ordered a drink. Then he noticed a seventy-year-old woman at the other end of the bar and he told the bartender to buy the lovely young lady a drink.

As the evening progressed, Morris joined the lady and they went back to her apartment, where they got it on.

Two days later, the old man noticed that he was developing a drip, and he headed for the rest home doctor.

After careful examination the doctor asked the old man if he had engaged in sex recently.

The old man said, "Sure!"

The doctor asked if he could remember who the woman was and where she lived.

"Sure . . . but why?"

The doctor said, "Well, you'd better get over there, you're about to come!"

On his wedding day, the groom walked down the aisle with a big grin on his face.

His best man said, "I know this is your wedding day but I've never seen you with such a big smile."

The groom whispered, "I just got the best blow job I've ever had."

As the bride walked down the aisle she also grinned from ear to ear.

Her bridesmaid said to her, "I know this is

the happiest day in your life but I have never seen you with a bigger smile."

To which the bride replied, "I've just given my last blow job."

———————————

It was the first day of school for the kindergarten class. As the teacher walked into the classroom, she noticed something written on the chalkboard: *T T T 1A.*

She looked at the children and said, "Who wrote this?"

Little Johnny raised his hand and said, "I did, teacher."

"Well, what does that mean, Johnny?" asked the teacher.

Johnny answerd, "It means, 'To the teacher, one apple,'" and with that, he gave the teacher an apple.

"Very good," said the teacher. "Thank you."

The next morning, the teacher walked into

the classroom and noticed, once again, some-thing written on the board. This time the chalkboard read: *T T T 1O*.

She asked the children, "Who wrote this?"

Then little Bobby answered, "I did, teacher."

The teacher said, "Well, Bobby, what does that mean?"

Bobby said, "It means, 'To the teacher, one orange,'" and he gave the teacher an orange.

"Very good, Bobby, thank you."

The next morning, she walked into the classroom, and noticed on the board: *F U C K I T*.

Disappointed, the teacher exclaimed, "Who wrote this!"

Then little Juanito raised his hand and said, "I did, teacher."

Angrily, the teacher asked, "Well, what does this mean, Juanito?"

"It means, 'From us Chicano kids, one tamale.'"

A man is walking along the beach when he spots a woman crying. She has no arms and no legs, but otherwise has a gorgeous body and a beautiful face.

He stops and asks her why she is crying.

She answers, "I just want someone to hug me."

So he leans over, picks her up, gives her a warm, tender hug, then sets her down again.

She thanks him, and he continues on his way.

Later that afternoon as he is walking back along the beach, he spots the woman again, who's still crying.

He asks her what's wrong now. She answers, "I just want someone to kiss me."

So he leans over, picks her up, gives her a long, passionate kiss, then sets her down again.

She thanks him, and he continues on his way.

Later that evening, he's finishing off yet another walk along the beach, and once again, he sees the woman, still crying.

He asks her what's wrong this time, and she answers, "I just want someone to fuck me."

So he leans over, picks her up, carries her down to the pier, walks down to the end of it, throws her off the edge, and shouts down to her, "Now you're fucked!"

––––––––––––––

What does an old lady have between her tits that a young lady doesn't?

Her belly button.

––––––––––––––

Why do women rub their eyes when they get up in the morning?

Because they don't have balls to scratch.

––––––––––––––

What's a Jewish American Princess's idea of natural childbirth?
Absolutely no makeup.

———————————

Why do Jewish American Princesses have crow's-feet?
From squinting and saying "Suck *what?*"

———————————

Did you hear about the Polish lesbian?
She loved men.

———————————

How do you starve a black man?
    Hide his food stamps in his work boots.

———————————

What do you get when you cross a Mexican
with a Vietnamese?
    A car thief who can't drive.

———————————

What do you call a guy with no arms and no
legs on the lawn all night?
    Dewey.

———————————

What's the similarity between Bill Clinton and a carpenter?

One screw in the wrong place and the whole cabinet falls apart.

A guy is swerving down the road and gets pulled over. The cop says, "You have to take a Breathalyzer test."

The guy says, "I can't. I have asthma, and it'll start me on a coughing fit."

The cop says, "Then I have to give you a blood test."

The guy says, "You can't. I'm a hemophiliac, and if you prick me, I'll bleed all over the place."

The cops says, "Then you have to get out of the car and walk a straight line."

The guy says, "I can't."

The cop says, "Why not?"

The guy says, "Because I'm drunk. Didn't you see the way I was driving, you asshole?"

———————

What is the leading cause of death among lesbians?

Hair balls.

———————

What's worse than finding a dead baby on your pillow in the morning?

Realizing you were drunk and made love to it the night before.

———————————

What's the difference between Michael Jackson and acne?

Acne doesn't come on your face until you're about fifteen.

———————————

Why do sumo wrestlers shave their legs?

They don't want to be mistaken for lesbians.

———————————

A World of Eerie Suspense
Awaits in Novels by Noel Hynd